QUTB
MINAR

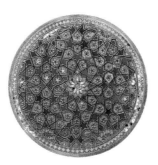

DORLING KINDERSLEY
London, New York, Munich,
Melbourne and Delhi

Head of Publishing	Aparna Sharma
Art Director	Shefali Upadhyay
Design Manager	Arunesh Talapatra
Designers	Neerja Rawat, Neha Ahuja
Editors	Dipali Singh, Ankush Saikia, Suchismita Banerjee
Production Manager	Pankaj Sharma
DTP Designers	Jagtar Singh, Dheeraj Arora Harish Aggarwal
Photographers	Amit Pasricha, Deepak Aggarwal

First published in India in 2008
by Dorling Kindersley (India) Pvt. Limited
in association with Penquin Book India (P) Ltd.,
11, Community Centre, Panchsheel Park, New Delhi - 110017
Copyright © 2008 Dorling Kindersley (India) Pvt. Limited

ISBN 978-0-14-306556-2

Printed and bound in
Gopsons Papers Ltd., Noida, India

Discover more at
www.dk.com

Discover more at
www.penguinbooksindia.com

QUTB
MINAR

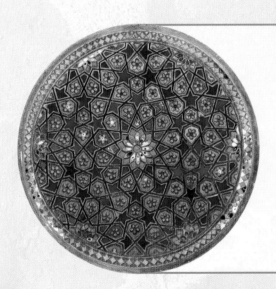

Tower of Triumph

Most human beings dream of being immortal, and this is particularly true of kings, whose desire to live on is reflected in the monuments they build. The Qutb Minar, a five-storeyed structure of sandstone and marble, reaches for the sky in just such an expression of imperial might. It is believed to have been built as a symbol of victory and to celebrate the establishment of the Delhi Sultanate in the newly conquered territory in India. Towering over the city of Delhi, it is the principal monument of the Qutb complex, which has been declared a UNESCO World Heritage Site. The monuments comprising this complex (the earliest examples of the Indo-Islamic architectural style) were built from the late 12th century onwards by the rulers of the Delhi Sultanate. They were built

⚜ MEDIEVAL MONUMENTS
The Qutb complex lies in the south of Delhi, the capital city of India.

over Qila Rai Pithora, a city founded by the Chauhan Rajput clan and the first of the fabled seven cities that made up Delhi (the others being Mehrauli, Siri, Tughlaqabad, Firozabad, Jahanpanah, and Shahjahanabad). The Chauhans were forced to cede it to Muhammad of Ghur in 1193. Qutbuddin Aibak, Muhammad's general, became the first sultan of Delhi and commenced the construction of the Qutb Minar (the word *qutb* means "axis", while *minar* means "tower"). The building of the tower cannot be attributed to a single ruler – Aibak died after completing just one storey, while the rest were added by subsequent kings. Surrounding the Minar is the Mehrauli area, which is steeped in history, with numerous monuments dotting the landscape.

Rulers of Delhi

Marking a new era in Indian history, the Delhi Sultanate was established in 1206. The Mamluk (formerly known as the Slave kings), the Khilji, Tughlaq, Sayyid, and Lodi sultans ruled successively for more than two centuries, changing the political and cultural milieu of the Indian subcontinent. The great Mughal empire followed. Its might declined rapidly in the early eighteenth century, leaving the way clear for the European powers. The British then gained control and rose as a political force; their forces dethroned the last Mughal emperor in 1857.

Given below are some important dates relating to the Qutb complex.

≫ 1206–1290 **Mamluk sultans**

1206–1210 Qutbuddin Aibak
1211–1236 Shamsuddin Iltutmish
1266–1286 Ghiyasuddin Balban

≫ 1290–1321 **Khilji sultans**

1296–1316 Alauddin Khilji

≫ 1321–1414 **Tughlaq sultans**

1351–1388 Firoz Shah Tughluq

≫ 1414–1451 **Sayyid sultans**

≫ 1451–1526 **Lodi sultans**

1488–1517 Sikander Lodi

≫ 1526–1857 **The Mughal emperors**

1526–1530 Zahiruddin Babur
1530–1556 Nasiruddin Humayun
1556–1605 Jalaluddin Akbar
1605–1717 The other Great Mughals
1836–1857 Bahadur Shah Zafar

Looking Back in Time

The strategic location of Delhi made it an attractive prospect for invaders from Central Asia. In 1193, Muhammad of Ghur (in what is now central Afghanistan) swept into north India and sacked Delhi, setting the stage for his general, Qutbuddin Aibak, to establish his rule in the city. The Delhi Sultanate expanded, surviving into the early 16th century. In 1526, another invader from Central Asia – Zahiruddin Babur – took over Delhi and laid the foundation of the Mughal empire that was to dominate the subcontinent for over 200 years.

MINARET OF JAM ≫
The Qutb Minar was inspired by a minaret – 65m (214ft) high – in the remote valley of Jam in western Afghanistan. This minaret was built between 1193 and 1194 by Ghiyasuddin, the sultan of Ghur (brother of Muhammad of Ghur).

The Mamluk sultans

The first Muslim rulers of India, the Mamluk sultans, reigned for 84 years. When Muhammad of Ghur died in 1206, Qutbuddin Aibak, a former slave, stayed on in Delhi and was crowned as the sultan. Shamsuddin Iltutmish, Aibak's son-in-law, and Ghiyasuddin Balban, both Il-bari Turks – were also slaves before they ascended the throne (their tombs lie in the Qutb complex). Iltutmish expanded the Delhi Sultanate till Sind in the west and Bengal in the east. Balban, the eighth sultan, ruled with an iron hand, quelling rebellions to bring peace to his kingdom. As the empire expanded, the sultans sought to demonstrate their power by building grand monuments around the Qutb Minar.

QUTB MINAR

ALAI DARWAZA

The Khilji rulers

Jalaluddin Khilji, who belonged to an Afghan tribe, wrested power from Balban's successors and established the Khilji dynasty. His nephew, Alauddin Khilji, was the next Khilji sultan. Aiming to conquer the whole of India, he launched successful expeditions against the rich kingdoms south of Delhi between 1299 and 1305 and extended the sultanate. His architectural vision was grandiose in conception, as evidenced by the unfinished Alai Minar (ambitiously begun as a gigantic rival of the Qutb Minar), the impressive Alai Darwaza, and the sizable extensions added to the Quwwat-ul-Islam Masjid built by Aibak.

balconied window

HAUZ KHAS MADRASA

The Tughlaq sultans

The first Tughlaq sultan was Ghiyasuddin Tughlaq, who established his capital at Tughlaqabad, the third of Delhi's seven cities. There were 11 rulers of the Tughluq dynasty, but only the first three generations were interested in architecture. Firoz Shah Tughlaq was a prolific builder who added the fourth and fifth storeys of the Qutb Minar and created his own city, Firozabad, in the north of Delhi, along the Yamuna river. He also built numerous rest houses and *madrasas* (schools). A *madrasa* and an L-shaped mosque built by him can be seen in Hauz Khas, Delhi.

The Lodis

The Sayyids contributed very little to the Qutb complex, but Sikander Lodi of the Lodi dynasty carried out repairs and restoration work of the Minar. Sikander Lodi's octagonal tomb lies in the Lodi Garden, Delhi.

Influences from afar

The new conquerors of northern India brought their own religious and social ideas with them. In architecture, too, they introduced new techniques of design. At the same time, the local craftsmen who were set to work on monuments for the new rulers managed to introduce indigenous elements in the structures. There was an initial stage where Hindu or Jain temples were destroyed and the material used for new buildings, as in the Quwwat-ul-Islam Masjid in the Qutb complex. Later, however, monuments were built from materials sourced from nearby places. One of the architectural features the Central Asian rulers brought with them was the true or keystone arch (below), which was an arch built with wedge-shaped stone blocks. Prior to this, the local craftsmen used corbelled or "false" arches.

CORBELLED OR FALSE ARCH

keystone

TRUE ARCH WITH KEYSTONE

⚜ TWO TYPES OF ARCHES
The corbelled arch was built by laying stones horizontally and rounding the edges at the top. It could not support extra weight on it, as can be seen in the Quwwat-ul-Islam Masjid screen. The true arch was first used in Balban's tomb, which lies some distance away from the complex.

Qutb Minar

The construction of this magnificent minaret was begun by Qutbuddin Aibak in the year 1199. When Aibak died in 1210, only the first storey of the Minar had been built. Iltutmish, Aibak's son-in-law, added three more storeys to it, and Firoz Shah Tughlaq added the fourth and fifth storeys in 1368 after a lightning strike knocked off the top of the Minar. Conceived of as a tower of victory and faith, the Minar might have also served as a look-out and as a place for the muezzin's call to prayer. But it was most likely intended as a symbol of the power of Delhi's new rulers.

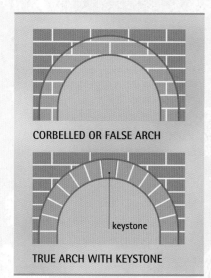

⚜ ARCHED ENTRANCE
The now-closed doorway leads to a spiral staircase with 379 steps to the top.

⚜ CALLIGRAPHIC BANDS AND FLUTINGS

The tapering shaft of the Minar is encircled by decorative bands engraved with historical information and verses from the Quran in the Naskh, or "copying", style of calligraphy. The first three storeys are fluted: alternate rounded and angular flutings (grooves) on the first storey, rounded ones on the second, and only angular flutings on the third.

Naskh lettering

rounded flutings

Aspects of the Minar

Standing 72.5m (238ft) tall, the Qutb Minar is one of the most perfect minarets ever built – and the tallest minaret in India. Its diameter at the base is 14.4m (47ft), tapering upwards to 2.75m (9ft). It was damaged by lightning in 1326, 1368, and 1503. A number of iron clamps were then added to reinforce the stone joints and to act as lightning conductors. The Minar tilts about 0.6m (2ft) towards the southwest, but this is not seen as a threat to the structure.

SMITH'S FOLLY

Major Robert Smith of the Royal Engineers added this *chhatri* (kiosk) atop the Minar in 1829 after the original cupola was struck by an earthquake. It was later removed, and came to be known as "Smith's Folly". It can be seen to the left of the main entry path.

✎ LATER ADDITIONS

There is a marked architectural difference in the top two storeys added by Firoz Shah Tughlaq, especially evident in the liberal use of marble. The marble bands are embellished with inscriptions carved in fine calligraphy.

balcony above alcoves

ornamental band

marble panelling

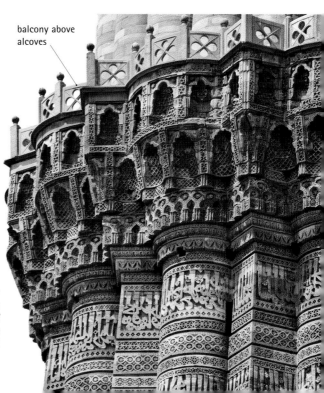

BALCONIES AND ORNATE BRACKETS ☞

The first three storeys of the Minar have projecting balconies, each opening out from the internal staircase, which are supported by elaborately carved muqarnas (stalactite brackets) above honeycomb patterned alcoves. These brackets were an architectural feature imported from the Arabic world.

Layout of the Qutb Minar Complex

The Qutb Minar and complex is the crowning architectural achievement of the Delhi Sultanate. Though called a "complex", it was not planned in a cohesive way. Various rulers added structures to it over the centuries following the conquest of northern India. Among other monuments, here are the Alai Darwaza, with Imam Zamin's Tomb right next to it, and the Quwwat-ul-Islam Masjid with its spectacular sandstone screen.

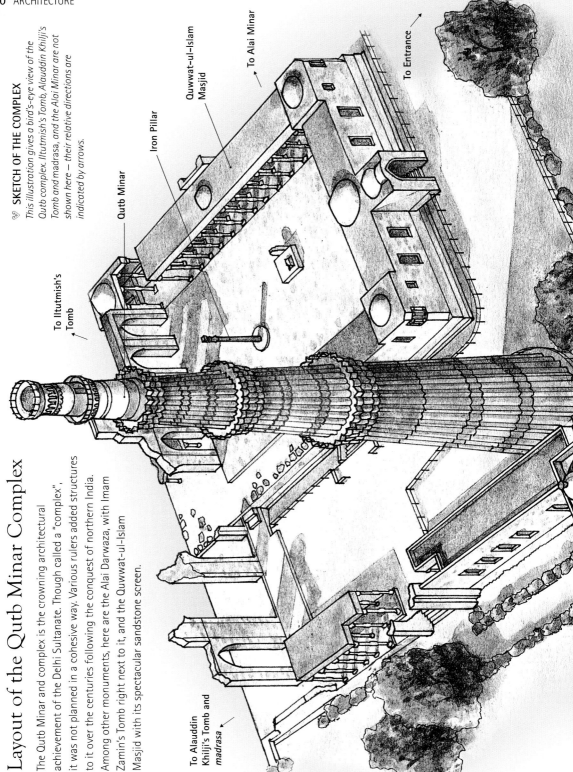

SKETCH OF THE COMPLEX
This illustration gives a bird's-eye view of the Qutb complex. Iltutmish's Tomb, Alauddin Khilji's Tomb and madrasa, and the Alai Minar are not shown here – their relative directions are indicated by arrows.

Qutb Minar

Iron Pillar

Quwwat-ul-Islam Masjid

To Alai Minar

To Entrance

To Iltutmish's Tomb

To Alauddin Khilji's Tomb and *madrasa*

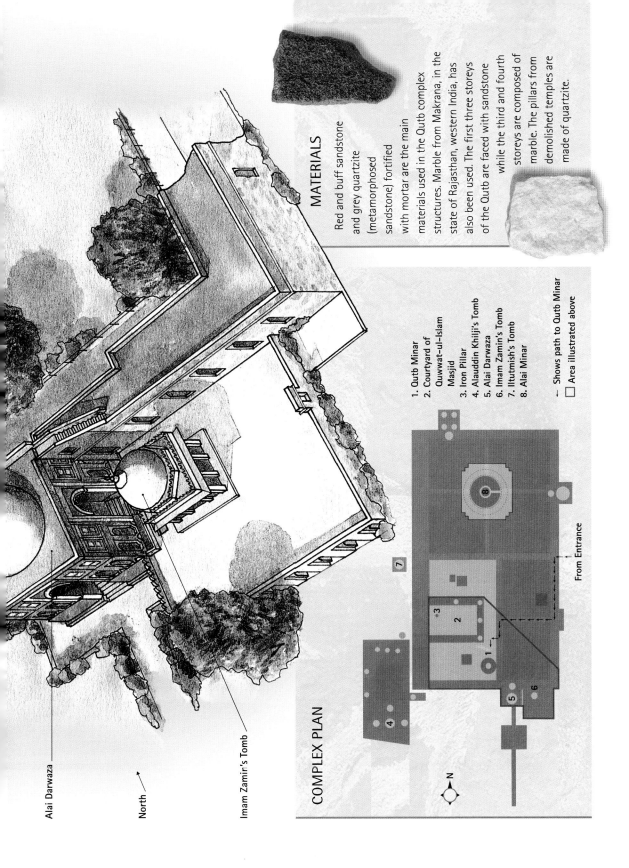

Alai Darwaza

North

Imam Zamin's Tomb

MATERIALS

Red and buff sandstone and grey quartzite (metamorphosed sandstone) fortified with mortar are the main materials used in the Qutb complex structures. Marble from Makrana, in the state of Rajasthan, western India, has also been used. The first three storeys of the Qutb are faced with sandstone while the third and fourth storeys are composed of marble. The pillars from demolished temples are made of quartzite.

COMPLEX PLAN

1. Qutb Minar
2. Courtyard of Quwwat-ul-Islam Masjid
3. Iron Pillar
4. Alauddin Khilji's Tomb
5. Alai Darwaza
6. Imam Zamin's Tomb
7. Iltutmish's Tomb
8. Alai Minar

→ Shows path to Qutb Minar
☐ Area illustrated above

From Entrance

N

PILLAR AND SCREEN
The maqsura or screen of the late 12th-century
Quwwat-ul-Islam Masjid forms a backdrop
for the famed fourth-century Iron Pillar. The red
sandstone screen is decorated with floral carvings
and calligraphy. The Iron Pillar is said to have been
brought to Qila Lal Pithora from central India by
Anangapal, a Rajput ruler of Delhi, and placed
with the group of 27 temples that stood there.

CLOISTERED COURTYARD
The mosque is built on the raised platform (reached by steep steps on the north, east, and west sides) of an earlier temple. The central courtyard, where people gathered to pray, is rectangular and measures 43 x 33m (141 x 108ft).

Quwwat-ul-Islam Masjid

Commissioned by Qutbuddin Aibak, the Quwwat-ul-Islam (Might of Islam) Masjid was the first congregational mosque to be built in India. Constructed between 1193 and 1197, the mosque consists of a courtyard enclosed by pillared cloisters on three sides and an elaborately decorated screen.

Standing tall at 7m (2ft) in the courtyard is the Iron Pillar. It bears an inscription describing it as a flagstaff of the Hindu deity Vishnu and commemorates King Chandragupta II, which dates it to the fourth-century Gupta period.

FUSION OF STYLES

Heralding a new architectural style combining Hindu and Islamic decorative elements, the mosque is composed of material taken from 27 demolished temples. Hindu motifs on the pillars, such as *ghata-pallava* (flower-pots), lotuses, and tasselled ropes, blend with Islamic calligraphy and patterns on the sandstone screen of the mosque.

ORNAMENTAL FLOWER-POT

PILLARED VERANDAH
The ornate pillars of the verandahs are square in shape, in the Hindu style.

FLORAL MOTIFS ON CEILING

THE IRON PILLAR
This pillar is composed of pure iron (98 per cent). A tribute to Indian metallurgy, it has shown almost no signs of rusting over the past 16 centuries.

Sandstone screen

Once the mosque was completed in 1197, a *maqsura*, a screen demarcating an enclosed prayer space, was constructed in front of the prayer hall by Aibak in 1199. Consisting of a main central arch flanked by smaller arches, it faces towards the west, the direction of Mecca. It is said to be modelled on the screen of Prophet Muhammad's mosque in Medina. Iltutmish and later, Alauddin Khilji, extended it to enclose the Qutb Minar and the Alai Minar.

ORNATE CALLIGRAPHY

⚜ GRAND ARCHES
The ogee-shaped (pointed) arches of the maqsura are lavishly ornamented with geometric and arabesque patterns as well as Quranic inscriptions.

⚜ SANSKRIT INSCRIPTION
Engraved on the iron pillar is an inscription in Sanskrit in the Gupta-Brahmi script mentioning King Chandragupta II.

Alai Darwaza

Remarkable for its perfect proportions and ornamented façade, the Alai Darwaza, built by Alauddin Khilji in 1311, stands to the southeast of the Qutb Minar. It was the only one of four planned gateways to the Minar that was actually built because Alauddin died in 1316, before he could complete the construction. The Darwaza is square in shape and has lofty doorways that are arched openings to the four main compass points. One of the earliest buildings to use the true arch, the structure features an external relief of inscriptional panels in marble, and decorative details in red sandstone. The central arch rises to nearly the whole height of the structure, its bands embellished with arabesque, geometric, and floral patterns. It is surmounted by a dome supported by recessed corner arches. Parts of the upper wall facing have come off, the square outline of the present parapet being the result of repair work carried out in 1828 by Major Robert Smith, a British military engineer.

DETAIL

❀ **WINDOW**
The windows of the Darwaza feature jaalis (latticed screens) set within arches. The lotus-bud fringe on the arch is characteristic of the Khilji period.

SCREEN FROM INTERIOR

wide dome

carved marble panels

⚶ GATEWAY TO THE MINAR
Inscriptions on the archways mention Alauddin's title, and record his extension of the Quwwat-ul-Islam Masjid in 1311.

A builder with visions of grandeur

Apart from constructing the impressive Alai Darwaza, Alauddin Khilji extended the Quwwat-ul-Islam Masjid's enclosure and screen and started the construction of the massive Alai Minar. The foundations of Siri, the second city of Delhi (and the first to be built by a Delhi sultan) were laid during his reign. He also built a *madrasa* and what would eventually be his tomb. Near Siri, he had a vast *hauz khas* (reservoir) built to supply water to his citadel.

✎ CONTRAST IN COLOURS
On the sides of the central arch are marble floral motifs offset by carved sandstone lotus-buds and twining stems; below is a richly patterned band in sandstone.

Imam Zamin's Tomb

Imam Zamin (his actual name was Muhammad Ali) was a 15th-century Sufi saint who came to Delhi from Turkestan during the reign of Sikander Lodi. He probably held a position of some importance in the Quwwat-ul-Islam Masjid. His tomb was built beside the eastern gateway of the Alai Darwaza during the reign of Mughal emperor Humayun, which makes it a later structure than the other monuments in the complex. The square building rises 16.5m (54ft) high and is decorated with marble panelling above the *chhajjas* (sloping eaves).

❧ MARBLE SLAB
An inscription in Naskh lettering above the doorway states that the saint built the tomb between 1537 and 1538, and died a year later.

SAINTLY AURA ❧
Marked by simplicity, this small structure bears a large dome on an octagonal base, topped by stepped battlements.

LATTICED SCREENS

The sandstone screens on three sides of the tomb filter the glare of sunshine. They stand out for their intricate geometrical patterns and star shapes.

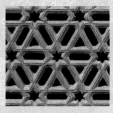

DESIGN DETAIL

INTERIOR 📝

The 12 pilasters inside Imam Zamin's tomb are connected by sandstone jaalis (latticed screens). Marble has been used for the sepulchre and for decorating the interior, particularly the richly carved mihrab (Mecca-facing prayer niche).

Alauddin's Madrasa and Tomb

The *madrasa* of Alauddin Khilji lies to the southwest of the Quwwat-ul-Islam Masjid. Built by Alauddin as a school to teach Islamic scripture, it is a complex of small chambers, some facing a quadrangular lawn. It is capped by high domes and the arches of the doorways are corbelled. To the south of the court is a large square structure, now in ruins, said to be the tomb of Alauddin; the remains of a projecting portico can be seen, but the dome that originally surmounted the tomb has vanished.

🔹 **ALAUDDIN'S RESTING PLACE**
The western wall of Alauddin Khilji's tomb has a small mihrab for offering prayers.

🔹 **SCHOOL AND SEPULCHRE**
The concept of a combined madrasa (below) and tomb (below left) is seen here for the first time in India.

Iltutmish's Tomb

Shamsuddin Iltutmish, the successor of Qutbuddin Aibak, built this tomb for himself in 1235. The tomb is located to the northwest of the Qutb complex, near Iltutmish's extensions to the Quwwat-ul-Islam Masjid. It was originally capped by a dome supported by "squinch arches", a type of true arch (see p.8), but this collapsed because the local artisans were unfamiliar with the technique of constructing true arches. The exterior walls are unornamented, relieved only by simple carved bands. In contrast, the interior is richly adorned with geometric and arabesque patterns as well as Quranic inscriptions in Naskh and Kufic lettering.

⊛ UNEMBELLISHED EXTERIOR
Each side of this tomb, a square structure with a plain façade, is 9m (29.5ft) in length. It has entrances on three sides, and was originally covered by a dome.

OPEN CHAMBER ⊰
The marble cenotaph lies in the middle of the open tomb chamber. The actual kabr or grave lies in the crypt, ringed by elaborately ornamented squinch arches.

⊱ CENTRAL MIHRAB
On the closed western wall are three mihrabs. The central one is made of marble, its arches, pillars, and panels decorated with geometrical and floral carvings.

squinch arch

❦ **RICHLY ORNAMENTED ARCHES**
*A profusion of carved calligraphic inscriptions
and floral patterns cover the three arched doorways
of Iltutmish's tomb; this offsets the simplicity of the
plain exterior walls.*

Alai Minar

A short walk away from the Quwwat-ul-Islam Masjid and Alauddin's
madrasa is the Alai Minar. This unfinished minaret (only the first storey
was constructed) was built by Alauddin Khilji around the year 1315.
Standing 24.5m (80ft) tall, it was intended to be twice the height and
size of the Qutb Minar – a part of his grand project of extending the
Quwwat-ul-Islam Masjid to twice its original size. Unlike the Qutb Minar,
it stands on a high platform or base. Work on the Minar was stopped
after Alauddin's death in 1316.

❦ **THE SECOND MINAR**
*This incomplete structure has angular flutings on
the outside, an entrance on the east, and a gently
sloping ramp on the inside. It gives an idea of how
the Qutb Minar looked when it was begun.*

incomplete base made
of sandstone rubble

Mehrauli

To the north, south, and west of the Qutb complex is the area that was once Lal Kot, the settlement built by the Tomar Rajputs. To the east, where the village of Lado Sarai now stands, is the area where the Chauhan Rajputs built their city of Qila Rai Pithora. Very little of either Lal Kot or Rai Pithora survive today.

At present, to the south of the Qutb complex lies the Mehrauli Archaeological Park of the Delhi Development Authority. It covers an expanse of more than 250 acres and contains the ruins of numerous monuments including mosques, tombs, water tanks, and gateways, dating from the 13th century through to the 19th century.

To the west of the Archaeological Park is Mehrauli. Once a tiny village, Mehrauli (derived from the name "Mihirapuri" – *mihir* means sun – indicating that a sun temple might once have existed here) has now grown into a bustling urban settlement. It has been inhabited more or less continuously since the Delhi Sultanate period, starting from around the end of the 12th century, till the present day.

⚘ LUSH GREENERY
A lawn in the Archaeological Park where visitors can relax in the peaceful surroundings.

Around the Qutb complex

A walk in the Mehrauli Archaeological Park and village is a reminder of the India of centuries ago. The remarkable monuments here range from the 13th-century Sultan Balban's Tomb, Jamali Kamali Mosque and Tomb, and the Dargah Qutb Sahib, to later structures such as Jahaz Mahal, Adham Khan's Tomb (built by Akbar), Muhammad Quli Khan's Tomb, and the Madhi Masjid.

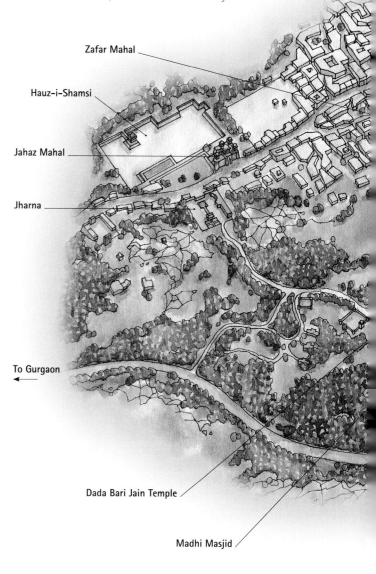

Zafar Mahal

Hauz–i–Shamsi

Jahaz Mahal

Jharna

To Gurgaon

Dada Bari Jain Temple

Madhi Masjid

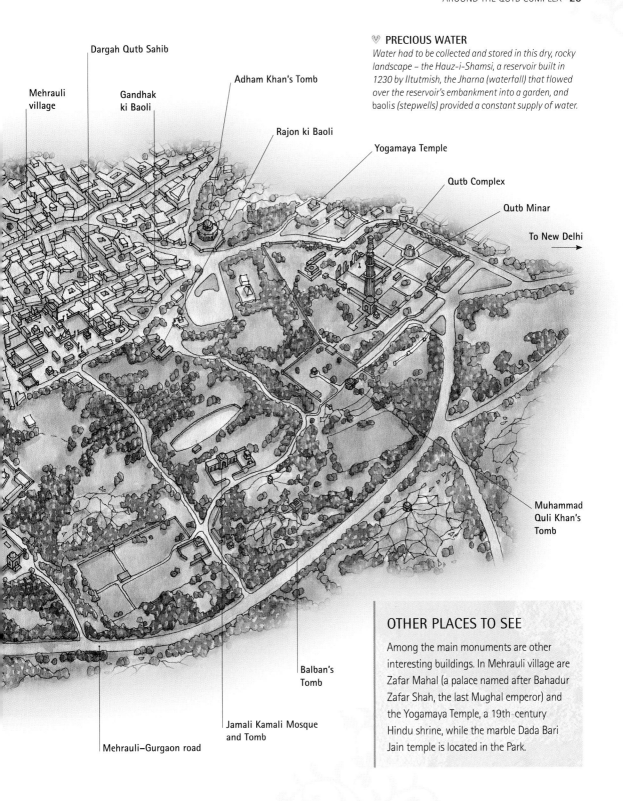

Dargah Qutb Sahib

Mehrauli
village

Gandhak
ki Baoli

Adham Khan's Tomb

Rajon ki Baoli

Yogamaya Temple

Qutb Complex

Qutb Minar

To New Delhi

Muhammad
Quli Khan's
Tomb

Balban's
Tomb

Jamali Kamali Mosque
and Tomb

Mehrauli–Gurgaon road

♥ PRECIOUS WATER

*Water had to be collected and stored in this dry, rocky
landscape – the Hauz-i-Shamsi, a reservoir built in
1230 by Iltutmish, the Jharna (waterfall) that flowed
over the reservoir's embankment into a garden, and
baolis (stepwells) provided a constant supply of water.*

OTHER PLACES TO SEE

Among the main monuments are other
interesting buildings. In Mehrauli village are
Zafar Mahal (a palace named after Bahadur
Zafar Shah, the last Mughal emperor) and
the Yogamaya Temple, a 19th-century
Hindu shrine, while the marble Dada Bari
Jain temple is located in the Park.

Jamali Kamali Mosque and Tomb

The elegant Jamali Kamali Mosque and Tomb lie within the Mehrauli Archaeological Park area. Sheikh Fazlullah, also known as Jamali, was a popular poet-saint during the reigns of Sikander Lodi and the Mughal emperor, Babur. Construction of the mosque and tomb began in 1528, and was completed during Humayun's reign. The prayer hall of the mosque has five arches, with two staircases leading up from it to the top of the mosque. Beside the mosque is an enclosure with a tomb, which houses two graves: the one in the centre is Jamali's, and the other is said to be of a person called Kamali, perhaps Jamali's brother

⚶ ENCLOSURE FOR THE GRAVES
The Jamali Kamali Tomb is a square, flat-roofed structure that lies in a courtyard, beside the mosque.

POETRY IN BLUE

The domed ceiling of the tomb is embellished with exquisite blue tiles in floral designs offset by incised plaster painted in red, ochre, and white; verses penned by Jamali are worked into the pattern.

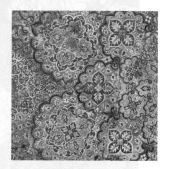

⚶ MOSQUE ENTRANCE
Carved bands and rosettes adorn the central arch.

⚶ ARCADED HALL
A succession of arches grace the mosque's prayer hall.

Balban's Tomb

Considerably restored, Balban's tomb is in the Archaeological Park, beside the Mehrauli–Gurgaon road. Balban's reign lasted almost to the end of the Mamluk rule in Delhi and his tomb was built in 1280. A square chamber with arched openings on all four sides, it was once crowned by a dome, which has collapsed. It is said that Balban died of grief when his son Muhammad, known as Khan Shahid, was killed in battle (a rectangular chamber located to the east of Balban's tomb is believed to be his tomb).

⚜ OPEN TO THE SKY
The rubble-built tomb of Balban lies in a clearing amidst thick undergrowth and is surrounded by ruins of the old Mehrauli village. The cenotaph itself is now unprotected by a roof.

⚜ FIRST TRUE ARCH
Marked by the ravages of time, but still standing intact are the arches of the tomb; they are the first true arches (see p.8) used in Indo-Islamic architecture.

Adham Khan's Tomb

This tomb stands atop a hillock just before the Mehrauli village. Octagonal in shape, the structure stands on a terrace enclosed by a wall with towers at the corners. It has a verandah with three arched openings on each side. Adham Khan was a general in the Mughal army and the son of Emperor Akbar's wet nurse, Mahim Anga. He was thrown off the ramparts of the Agra Fort on Akbar's orders as a punishment for murdering Ataga Khan, the prime minister. It was in repentance for this act that Akbar built the tomb in 1562 for him and Mahim Anga, who died of grief when her son was killed. It is also known as the Bhul Bhulaiyan, or labyrinth, because a maze (now closed) lies within the tomb's walls.

ARCHES OF ADHAM KHAN'S TOMB

⚜ FLIGHT OF STEPS
An arch supports the steps to the terrace of Adham Khan's tomb.

❧ ORNATE PATTERNS
Capped by a dome, Quli Khan's tomb bears ornamental carvings and glazed tiles on its façade.

Quli Khan's Tomb

Rising from a high platform in a garden southeast of the Minar, is the octagonal tomb of Muhammad Quli Khan (Adham Khan's brother). In the 1840s, Thomas Metcalfe, British Resident at the Mughal Court, made it his summer retreat, naming it "Dilkusha" after he built chambers around it (he used the main tomb area as his dining room!).

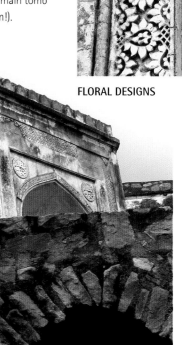

FLORAL DESIGNS

carvings on arch

The Baolis

Two *baolis* or step-wells lie close to the Qutb complex. In the Mehrauli Archaeological Park is the Rajon ki Bains *baoli* – it is so called because it was used by *rajs* (masons) long ago. A mosque stands at one side, where a *chhatri* (kiosk or pavilion with an umbrella-shaped dome) bears an inscription from 1506 mentioning that the structure was built during Sikander Lodi's reign. The Gandhak ki Baoli is a five-tier step-well in Mehrauli village. It was built in the 13th century during the reign of Iltutmish, and its *gandhak* (sulphur) waters were supposed to have healing properties.

⚜ ENTRANCE TO RAJON KI BAINS
A domed pavilion stands at the entrance of the baoli; the vestiges of blue tiles that circled the dome are still visible.

square pillars

⚜ GANDHAK KI BAOLI
Originally fed by a sulphur spring that emitted a strong smell, this baoli has a circular well at one end, reached by a flight of steps.

⚜ RAJON KI BAINS
This oblong baoli is built in four storeys – the upper storeys have arcades supported by piers, while the lowest one has deeply recessed arches.

colonnaded galleries

ⓐ **ORNATE PAVILION**
The saint's grave is sheltered by a newly built pavilion.

Dargah Qutb Sahib

The *dargah* or shrine of Qutbuddin Bakhtyar Kaki lies off a lane leading from the Mehrauli bazaar. A Sufi saint (the name "Kaki" comes from *kaks*, the small cakes he would eat during his fasts), he was born in Ush in Persia, and after travelling through Khurasan and Baghdad, came to India with the earliest Muslim conquerors. In India, he became a spiritual successor to the Sufi saint, Khwaja Moinuddin Chisthi of Ajmer, and preached during the reign of Iltutmish. He died in 1236 and his tomb lies inside the shrine, beneath a rectangular domed pavilion studded with mirrors.

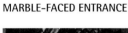

MARBLE-FACED ENTRANCE

DARGAH DOORWAY

ⓢ **PILLARED ENCLOSURE**
Only men are allowed to approach the tomb of the saint in the enclosure: women have to view it from behind a marble screen.

Hauz-i-Shamsi

The Hauz-i-Shamsi is a large *hauz,* a rainwater-fed tank, on the southern outskirts of Mehrauli, beyond the bazaar. It was built around 1230 by Sultan Iltutmish when, according to a legend, the Prophet Mohammed appeared to him in a dream and told him where to build the tank. The next morning the sultan visited the site and noticed a hoofprint, believed to have been that of the Prophet's horse. He had the tank excavated and a red sandstone domed pavilion with 12 pillars built at the site (with a stone marking the hoofprint). The pavilion is at the southwest corner of the tank.

PAVILION OVERLOOKING HAUZ-I-SHAMSI

Jahaz Mahal

At the northeast corner of the Hauz-i-Shamsi is the Jahaz Mahal, made of red and grey sandstone and probably built during the Lodi period. It consists of arched chambers enclosing a rectangular courtyard. Its location on the fringes of the tank gave it the name of Jahaz (Ship) Mahal as it appears to float on water. The Mahal may have served as a resthouse for pilgrims, but a *mihrab* on its western wall suggests that part of it was a mosque.

PALACE WALLS
Finely carved chhatris, studded with vestiges of bright blue tiles, stand atop each corner of the palace's walls.

glazed blue tiles

⚜ ENTRANCE
Flanking the arched entrance are small canopied balconies.

⚜ STEPPED ARCH
The exit gateway has a corbelled or stepped arch.

blue tiles

ORNAMENTAL DETAIL

Madhi Masjid

In the Archaeological Park, on a path off the main Mehrauli–Gurgaon road, is the Madhi Masjid. It is a simple but impressive double-storeyed mosque built during the Lodi or early Mughal period. The square gateway on the eastern side is made of grey stone, with projecting windows of red sandstone, and leads up to a courtyard. The three-arched prayer hall, which combines the features of a covered and an open wall-mosque, is profusely ornamented.

♥ OPEN COURTYARD
The thick, high walls enclosing the large courtyard are capped by parapets, making the mosque appear like a fortress.

Tourist information

By Air: For international travellers, the airport in Delhi is the Indira Gandhi International Airport. Travellers within India can avail of flights to and from the domestic terminal of the IGI Airport. For enquiries, visit www.delhi-tourism-india.com/ delhi-info. **By Rail:** Delhi is connected to all cities in India by the Indian Railways. For enquiries, visit www.indianrail.gov.in. **By Road:** Delhi is connected to all cities in India by road. **To get to the Qutb complex:** Autorickshaws, taxis, and luxury coaches are available for hire. For enquiries, visit www.delhitourism.nic.in.

Visitor's checklist

The best time to visit Delhi is between October and March. The Qutb complex is open to visitors from 6am to 6pm every day. The entrance fee for citizens of India and SAARC countries is Rs 10 per head, and US $5 or Rs 250 for visitors from other countries. Photography is permitted in the Qutb complex so do take your camera along. For updates on fees and timings, visit www.delhi-tourism-india.com/delhi-info.

Here are a few things you need to carry when travelling in India.

- Drinking water, torch, map or guidebook, mosquito repellent, loose change, sunblock
- First aid kit, medication for tropical diseases, such as diarrhoea, dysentery, and malaria; water purification tablets
- Light cotton clothes in summer; woollens in winter; hat, umbrella, or raincoat, easy-to-remove footwear
- Credit cards or travellers' cheques (optional, but advisable).

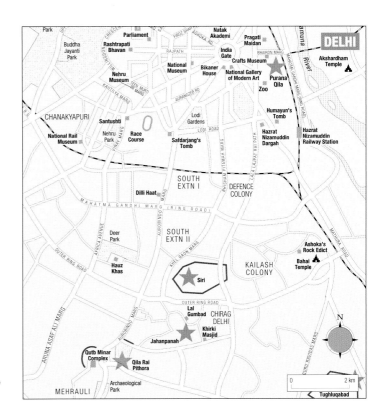

Publisher's acknowledgements

Dorling Kindersley and Penguin Books India would like to thank the following people for their help and guidance in preparing this book:
Dr Narayani Gupta and Ranjana Sengupta for reviewing the text so painstakingly; Punita Singh, Manager, Rough Guides India, for getting us permission to use the maps in the book; Jayaprakash Mishra of Rough Guides India and Suresh Kumar of DK Travel Guides for helping us with the maps.

Notes